The Bridegroom

Also translated by Antony Wood and published by
Angel Books:

Alexander Pushkin *Mozart and Salieri: The Little Tragedies*

ALEXANDER
PUSHKIN

The Bridegroom

WITH
Count Nulin

AND
The Tale of the Golden Cockerel

Translated with an afterword by
ANTONY WOOD

ANGEL BOOKS
London

To the memory of my father
with his precise sense of language
and of everything else

First published in 2002 by
Angel Books, 3 Kelross Road, London N5 2QS

British Library Cataloguing in Publication Data:
A catalogue record for this book is available from the British Library

ISBN 0–946162–67–0
ISBN 0–946162–68–9 pbk

Designed and typeset in Monotype Fournier by Derek Brown of
Oblong Creative Ltd, Wetherby

Printed in Great Britain by Bookcraft Ltd, Midsomer Norton on
Windrush Book Wove paper and bound by them

Contents

Acknowledgements

I AM VERY GRATEFUL to Mark Cohen, Peter France, Alla Gelich, James Greene, Bernard Johnson, Yuri Kleiner and Stanley Mitchell for their comments on individual poems; to Angela Livingstone who read successive drafts of two of the poems and with whom much was discussed; and to John Fuller and Christopher Logue, who made me put in more work at a late stage. To my wife Hazel I owe more than I can say for her continuous scrutiny, robust comments, and astonishing patience.

I should like to thank Marita Crawley for her kind donation on behalf of the British Pushkin Bicentennial Trust.

The illustrations
The drawing by Roman Pisarev (pen and ink) reproduced on page 8 was commissioned for this book.

A drawing by N. V. Kuz'min (pen and China ink, 1957) is reproduced on page 18 by permission of the National Pushkin Museum, St Petersburg. It is one of a set illustrating an edition of *Graf Nulin* published in 1957.

An etching depicting the palace of Tsar Dadon by K. V. Kuznetsov (dating from the 1930s) is reproduced on page 34 by permission of the State Pushkin Museum, Moscow. The original is in colour.

Detail of a portrait of Pushkin at Boldino by V. A. Serov (pencil and watercolour) is reproduced on the cover by permission of the National Pushkin Museum, St Petersburg. This portrait was undertaken for the Centenary Edition of the Works of Pushkin edited by P. P. Konchalovsky, published in Moscow in 1899, and was reproduced in the first volume.

Grateful acknowledgement is made to the museums mentioned above for supplying photographic material and for permission to reproduce it.

On pages 9, 19, 35 and 59 detail chosen at random from drawings by Pushkin in his notebooks is reproduced by permission of the Institute of Russian Literature, Russian Academy of Sciences, St Petersburg.

A. W.

The Bridegroom

FOR three whole days the merchant's daughter,
    Natasha, disappeared;
The third night came: in wild disorder
    Natasha reappeared.
Mother and father plied their questions,
Tried to bring about confessions.
    Natasha doesn't hear,
    She scarcely breathes from fear.

Her mother grieved, her father grieved,
    Long did they catechise her,
But when at last she was reprieved
    They still were none the wiser.
Natasha won back cheer and health,
Soon she was her former self
    And with her sisters sat
    Outside the shingle-gate.

There she is with her companions
    Beside the gate one day,
The merchant's girl, when all at once
    A troika gallops by.
Its young and dashing driver tugs
The reins of horses wrapped with rugs;
    He stands up in his sleigh,
    He'll crush what's in his way.

He glances at her as he drives,
    Natasha glances back,
On like the wind he whirls, he leaves
    Natasha thunderstruck.
Back to the house headlong she flies.
"I recognized him – him!" she cries –
    "I know that it was him!
    Stop him, save me from him!"

Shaking their heads, the family gather
    And listen full of gloom;
"Daughter dear," begins the father,
    "Tell me the truth now, come:
If someone has offended you,
Give us some sign, and that will do."
    Natasha doesn't speak.
    All she can do is weep.

Next day, betimes, a matchmaker
    Is waiting in the parlour.
She utters praises for Natasha,
    Then turns towards the father:
"We're buying – you've the goods for us,
And handsome is as handsome does:
    The lad has strength and style,
    He's free of guile and bile.

"He's wealthy, and he's also clever,
    He doesn't touch his cap,
Lives like a boyar, lacked he's never,
    Luck falls into his lap;
He'll have a mind to give the girl
A fox-fur coat, a precious pearl,
    Gold rings and necklaces
    And rich-brocaded dresses.

"He passed your gateway yesterday;
    He isn't one that dithers,
So let's to church now – what do you say?
    And take the icons with us?"
She sits and eats a plate of pie,
She talks with sighs and slanted eye,
    And what the poor bride hears
    Rouses her deepest fears.

"It's settled, then," agrees the father,
        "Aren't you the lucky one?
My dear Natasha, to the altar!
        It's dull to sit alone.
To go through life unwed is wrong,
The linnet has to leave off song,
        It's time to build a nest,
        Have children and be blessed."

Natasha leans against the wall,
        She tries to speak — instead
Begins to sob and shake and wail,
        Laugh as though off her head.
The matchmaker, in the disorder,
Runs to her with a flask of water —
        A gulp — and then a jet
        Over Natasha's head.

A family in calamity ...
        Natasha now comes to:
"Your will is sacred, I shall be
        Obedient to you.
Call my bridegroom to the feast,
Bake for a hundred guests at least,
        Make mead that's good and strong,
        And bring the law along."

"We shall now, angel of my heart!
    I'd place your happiness
Before my life!" At once they start,
    They bake their very best.
And now the worthy guests assemble,
And see, the bride is led to table;
    The bridesmaids weep and sing –
    A sleigh comes galloping.

The groom! Now everyone is present.
    The goblets clash and clink,
The loving-cup is found most pleasant;
    Guests take their fill of drink.
BRIDEGROOM:
"Dear friends, I must be satisfied:
Why does my own and fairest bride
    Not drink, nor eat, nor serve?
    Why does my fair bride grieve?"

"I'll tell you all I have to tell,"
    To the bridegroom spoke the bride.
"My life is now a life in hell,
    I weep all day and night.
An evil dream oppresses me."
The father: "What can this dream be?
    Dear daughter, if you please,
    Put our minds at ease."

"My dream was this", she spoke out loud.
    "I wandered in a wood,
At night; behind a bank of cloud
    A half-moon dimly stood;
I'd lost my path, and all around
No living soul, no living sound,
    Nothing at all that stirs,
    Only the tops of firs.

"And suddenly, as if I woke,
    I saw, close by, a hut.
I knocked – no answer. Then I spoke –
    The door stayed firmly shut.
I opened it, prayed, and went inside:
A candle burned, and in its light –
    Gold, silver, everywhere ...
    All shining, sumptuous ware."

BRIDEGROOM:
"How is your dream an evil one,
    Foretelling wealth untold?"
BRIDE:
"Wait, sir, till my account is done.
    On silver and on gold,
And cloths and carpets and brocade,
And silken stuffs from Novgorod –
    On marvels heaven-sent
    I gazed in wonderment.

"Then I heard shouts, and clop clop clop ...
    Up to the porch they drove.
I slammed the door – a single hop –
    I hid behind the stove.
Soon many voices once again ...
Into the hut tramped twelve young men,
    And with them was a maiden,
    A pure and lovely maiden.

"They entered in a noisy horde,
    And none took off his hat;
To table, icons quite ignored,
    Without a grace they sat,
The eldest brother at their head,
The youngest brother on his right,
    And on his left the maiden,
    The pure and lovely maiden.

"Laughter and clamour, singing, yelling,
    Unbridled merriment ..."
BRIDEGROOM:
"How can your dream be bad, foretelling
    Good fortune and content?"
BRIDE:
"Wait sir, till my account is done.
The din and revelry went on,
    The merriment was mad,
    Only the maid was sad.

"She spoke no word, she sat in grief,
    Would take no food, no mead.
The eldest brother grasped his knife
    And whistling, whetted it;
He glanced towards the lovely maid,
He gripped her swiftly by the braid,
    The villain killed her and
    Cut off her right hand."

The bridegroom, with a shrug, replied:
    "But this is downright drivel!
You mustn't grieve, beloved bride,
    Your dream cannot mean evil."
The bride is swift to answer him:
"Whose hand does it come from, then, this
       ring?" –
    Looks him full in the face;
    Each guest starts from his place.

The ring rolls clinking on the floor,
    The bridegroom has turned pale;
All is confusion. – Speaks the law:
    "Bind the criminal!"
Fettered, the villain was condemned
Without delay and met his end.
    Natasha's was the glory!
    And that is all our story.

Count Nulin

TIME to be off! Loud blows the horn;
The whippers-in in hunting dress
Have mounted promptly with the dawn,
The close-leashed borzois prance and press.
The master of the house appears,
And pausing in the porch awhile
He looks about; his visage bears
A broad, proprietorial smile.
He wears a girded Cossack coat
In which a Turkish knife is stowed,
A rum-flask hangs below his throat,
A horn upon a bronzen chain.
His night-clad wife, with sleepy eyes,
Looks from her window, vexed, it's plain,
By canine din and huntsmen's cries . . .
They bring the master of the house
His mount; he grabs the withers, gets
Foot firmly in the stirrup, shouts
Not to wait up – and off he sets.

The period to September's close
(To use the lowly terms of prose)
Can drive the country-dweller mad:
The wind, the sleet, the mud, the haze,
The howl of wolves – but then how glad
The hunter! Scorning easy ways
He thunders through remote terrain,
Spends nights in every kind of place,
Curses, gets soaked and chilled in rain,
Toasts the annihilating chase.

What, now, can occupy the spouse
Forsaken by the other spouse?
Not hard to find activities:
She must salt mushrooms, feed the geese,
Make sure the kitchen tasks are heeded,
Inspect the cellar and the barn –
Mistress's eye is always needed
To see that nothing comes to harm.

I'm sad to say, our heroine ...
(Oh dear! I quite forgot to name her:
"Natasha" she had always been,
But let us properly proclaim her
Natalya Pavlovna) ... I fear
That our Natalya Pavlovna
Had absolutely no idea
What her domestic duties were;

Her childhood had been spent, alas,
Not under sound paternal rule
But at a gentle boarding school
Run by a Madame Falbalas.

Upon a window-seat she sits,
Holding opened on her knees
A sentimental novel; it's
The Love of Armand and Élise:
Two-sided Family Correspondence,
Volume the Fourth – a classical,
Old-fashioned, long, long, long, long novel,
All moral and respectable,
With none of that Romantic nonsense.

At first Natalya Pavlovna
Had read this epic all agog,
But soon a fight distracted her
Between a yard-goat and a dog.
Boys gathered round with many a hoot.
Meanwhile, a turkey flock pursued
A sodden cockerel, gravely gobbling;
Around a pool three ducks went hobbling,
Then paddled in, and splashed and rolled;
A peasant-woman crossed the mud
To hang a pile of washing out.
It presently grew very cold –

Soon there'd be snow upon the ground ...
Then suddenly, a coach-bell's sound.

He who has lived the life apart
In rural gloom, my friends, knows well
How strongly it can stir the heart,
That jingle of a distant bell.
A friend come visiting at last,
Some comrade from our dashing past?
It surely can't be *her*? ... Good lord!
Nearer, nearer ... The heart beats loud ...
But further, further fades the sound,
And dies; the listener is ignored.

Natalya Pavlovna with glee
Runs quickly to the balcony:
Over the river, past the mill
A carriage speeds towards her – oh!
Crosses the bridge, draws nearer – no,
Turns left. Near tears, she gazes still.

But – joy! – an unexpected slope –
The carriage topples. "Filka, Vash!
Where are you? Quick, there's been a crash!
Ask them in at once. I hope
The gentleman will dine with me!
Is he alive? Do run and see,
Be quick!"

The servant hurries out.
And now our heroine flies about,
Throws on a shawl, fluffs up her hair,
Adjusts a curtain, moves a chair,
And waits. "Dear God, please bring them here."
At last, at long last, they appear.
Bespattered with the journey's dirt,
Somehow, severely bruised and hurt,
The sorry carriage crawls along.
Behind, a youthful gentleman
Limps. His undaunted serving-man,
A Frenchman, cries: "*Courage, allons!*"
They reach the porch, now here they are
Inside the house. Dear reader, while
A bedroom is prepared in style,
Its door is opened wide, Picard
Bustles about and mutters oaths,
His master seeks a change of clothes –
Let me describe the visitor.
Count Nulin, home from foreign tour,
Has squandered his inheritance
In fashionable extravagance.
He's on his way to Petropole
For show like some rare animal,
With store of hats and fans and waistcoats,
Cufflinks and corsets, cloaks and dress-coats,
Pins, studs and stockings à la mode,
Handkerchiefs with coloured edges,

Lorgnettes, a book of wicked sketches,
Guizot's new volume (utter rot!),
A novel by Sir Walter Scott –
And then the Paris Court's bons mots,
The latest song by Béranger,
Arias from Rossini, Paër,
And so on and so forth – you know.

Supper was laid a while ago;
Impatiently the hostess sighs.
Enter, at last, the visitor.
Up starts Natalya Pavlovna;
Solicitously she enquires:
His leg now, does it hurt to touch?
Oh, says the count, it's nothing much.
To table then without ado.
The count moves his place nearer hers,
And starts the conversation: first
He curses Holy Russia – who
Can live in such perpetual snow?
He misses life in Paris so . . .
"How is the theatre?" "In decline,
C'est bien mauvais, ça fait pitié.
Talma's quite deaf, his voice – a whine,
And Mamselle Mars shows every sign . . .
But then Potier, *le grand Potier!*
He is the most admired by far,
As much as he has ever been."

"Which writers are most popular?"
"Oh, d'Arlincourt and Lamartine."
"In Russia too they're imitated."
"Is that so? Then the Russian mind
Is really not so far behind?
God grant we'll soon be educated."
"Where is the waist-line?" "Very low –
Almost to ... This is now the line.
But your *toilette* – it's very fine:
These ruches, bows, and this design ...
All very much the mode, you know."
"We take the *Moscow Telegraph*."
"Oh, really? ... Would you care for some
Vaudeville? This will make you laugh."
The count proceeds to sing. "Count, come,
Please help yourself." "No more, I can't."

They rise. The hostess is in bliss.
Paris forgotten now, the count
Marvels at her: how sweet she is!
The evening passes quickly by;
The count is quite beside himself;
His hostess's expressive eye
Now warms, now sinks in mute reply ...
And all too soon the clock strikes twelve.
His man snores in the portico,
The neighbour's cockerel starts to crow,
The watchman strikes his iron bar,

All candles in the room are spent.
Rising, Natalya Pavlovna
Declares the evening at an end,
Wishes the count a good night's rest.
The dizzy, disappointed guest
Kisses her hand ... And now, guess what!
Where will coquetry end? The tease –
And may she be forgiven by God –
Gives the count's hand a gentle squeeze.

Natalya Pavlovna undresses;
Parasha stands behind her chair.
To this Parasha she confesses
Her every daily thought and care:
Parasha washes, sews, brings news,
Is grateful for cast-off fichus,
Provokes her master into laughter
And rails at him the moment after,
Lies to her mistress brazenly.
Now she holds forth impressively
About the count and his affairs;
The thorough knowledge that she airs!
Heaven knows where she has it from.
At last her mistress, with a frown –
"That's enough of your going on!" –
Demands her night-clothes, then lies down
And tells Parasha to be gone.

Meanwhile the count retires to rest;
Helped by his man, he gets undressed ...
Climbs into bed. Monsieur Picard
Offers his master a cigar,
A silver tumbler and a bottle,
Lamp, tweezers, clock and uncut novel.

In bed, our hero runs his eyes
Over a page of Walter Scott.
He grasps, however, not a jot,
Distracted by a wild surmise ...
"Can it be possible that I'm
In love," he wonders, "one more time?
How entertaining that would be,
What an adventure, what delight!
My hostess likes the look of me ..."
Nulin extingishes the light.

But sleep just will not come to him;
A fever runs through every limb.
The Devil fills his wakeful mind
With fancies of a sinful kind.
Our ardent hero with a sigh
Imagines that vivacious eye,
That rather full and rounded figure,
That voice's pleasing female flow,
That face's rosy country glow –
Finer than paint are health and vigour.

And oh! that shapely little foot,
And oh! the simple way she put
Her hand in his, and lightly squeezed!
The moment ought to have been seized –
How foolish to have left her. But
Time yet. Her door will not be shut ...
Donning his striped silk dressing-gown,
The count is speedily abroad.
In the dark a chair goes down;
Tarquin, in hope of sweet reward,
Once more sets forth to seek Lucretia,
Resolved to hazard all to reach her.

Thus you may see a cunning tom,
The mincing darling of the house,
Slip from the stove to stalk a mouse,
Creep stealthily and slowly on
Towards his victim, grow slit-eyed
And wave his tail from side to side,
Coil to a ball, extend his claws
And snap! – the wretch is in his paws.

On through the darkness groped the count
With passion burning in his breast,
Scarcely daring to draw breath
And trembling at each sudden sound
The floor-boards gave. At last he found
The sanctum door; a gentle press

Upon the stout brass handle – yes!
Slowly, softly the door uncloses ...
Inside the bedroom, fitfully
A lamp still burns, and palely glows as
The mistress peacefully reposes,
Asleep, or she pretends to be.

He enters, half-withdraws, and sighs –
Falls at her feet at last ... I urge
You ladies of St Petersburg:
Picture the wild awakening eyes
Of my Natalya Pavlovna –
What shall she do? Decide for her.

She stared in sheer bewilderment;
Our hero showered her with grand,
If imitative, sentiment,
And coolly his audacious hand
Reached out to touch her eiderdown.
At first she was too numbed to frown ...
Then realization dawned upon her,
And full of fury for her honour,
Also, we may suppose, of fear,
With sure and swiftly swinging hand
She didn't hesitate to land
A good hard blow on Tarquin's ear!

Count Nulin burned with deepest shame
At such an insult to his name.

I wonder how things might have gone,
The cut to self-esteem so deep,
Had not the barking of the pom
Woken Parasha from her sleep.
He heard her footsteps drawing close,
He cursed his refuge of the night,
The wilful beauty, and he rose
To take shamefaced and rapid flight.

How the assorted company
Spent the remainder of the night –
I'll leave imaginations free,
I don't intend to say who's right.

Comes morning. Taciturn, our guest
Rises and lazily gets dressed;
Carelessly, yawning, trims his nails,
Clumsily ties his kerchief, fails
To smooth moist locks. A call to tea
Breaks in upon his reverie.
What should he do? He strives to bury
His painful shame and secret fury,
And leaves the room.

His hostess dips
Her mischievous and mocking eyes
And, biting pretty scarlet lips,
In various wary ways she tries

A conversation. Shy and cold
At first, our hero grows more bold,
He gives his answers with a smile
And banters with a pleasant art;
Within a very little while
He has once more half-lost his heart.
There comes a clamour from the hall.
Who's there? "Natasha!"

     "Heavens above! ...
This is my husband, count. My love,
Count Nulin."

    "Glad to have you call ...
What nasty weather, my, it's raw ...
I passed the forge just now and saw
Your carriage – excellent repair.
Natasha dear! We caught a hare
Outside the orchard ... Vodka now!
It's not from these parts, count, you know –
I'll fetch you some, if you'll allow ...
You'll lunch with us before you go?"
"Well, I don't know, I mustn't stay."
"No, count, you mustn't be away,
My wife and I are glad of guests.
Do stay!"

   But still the count requests
They let him leave. His hopes are gone,
He is both furious and forlorn.
Picard, well strengthened by a glass,

Grunts with a heavy travelling-case;
Two servants hurry out to lash
The trunk upon the equipage
Now drawn up ready at the door;
Picard has seen to everything;
The count departs at last. What more
Can I relate? A word, my friends,
To add before my story ends.

Off, then, our hero's carriage rolled.
Natalya Pavlovna soon told
Her husband, neighbours, everyone
Just how my count had made so bold.
And who laughed more than anyone
To hear Natalya Pavlovna?
You'll never guess. – Why ever not?
Her husband! – No sir. Of the lot,
He was the least amused by far;
He called the count a fool, a whelp,
He'd vouch for it, he'd make him yelp,
He'd raise his pack of hounds to help.
No, he who laughed most heartily –
Their neighbour Lidin, twenty-three.

I think we may now truly say:
Fidelity need not give rise
(Not even, my dear friends, today)
To any very great surprise.

The Tale of the
Golden Cockerel

In the far-off Thrice-Ninth Clime,
In the Thrice-Eleventh Time,
Reigned the glorious Tsar Dadon.
Formidable from boyhood on,
He would unrelentingly
Cause offence and injury;
When, however, he grew old,
His campaigns were not so bold,
He desired a rest from war.
Then his neighbours by the score
Shook the tsar from his repose,
Dealt him many fearful blows.
Every outpost sent alarms;
Men in thousands under arms
He was driven to maintain,
Guarding his besieged terrain.
Generals did what they could do;
Hopeless, they were far too few:
Danger from the south they guessed –

In came raiders from the west;
Mended one catastrophe –
Evil visitors by sea.
Tears of rage shed Tsar Dadon,
Sleepless nights had turned him wan.
What a life, in such despair!
Seeking counsel everywhere,
An astrologer the monarch
Chose from his wise men, a eunuch;
Sent for him by courier.

And without delay the seer
Came before Dadon; he took
From his bag a golden cock.
Thus he spoke before his sire:
"Set this cockerel on a spire;
He will keep good watch for you,
This my golden bird and true:
When he sees it's quiet all round
He will sit without a sound;
But should ever foe be spied
Creeping up on any side,
An approaching armoured horde,
Something, somewhere, untoward –
Then my golden bird will rise,
Raise his comb toward the skies,
Ruffle up his plumes and crow:

He will turn towards the foe."
Tsar Dadon, at last consoled,
Promised quantities of gold.
"For the service you have done,"
To the eunuch glad Dadon,
"Whatsoever is your will
As my own I shall fulfil."

So the cock with faithful eye
Watched the frontiers from on high.
Danger spied, he'd stir and shuffle,
Face the foe with plumes a-ruffle:
"Now Tsar – cock-a doodle-do! –
What an easy life for you!"
And the neighbours of Dadon,
Soundly beaten one by one,
Once more held the tsar in awe:
By and by they ceased to war.

Two years passed; without a sound
Sat the cockerel; calm all round.
Then one day a mighty rumpus
Roused the ruler from his slumbers.
"Father of the people! Save us!"
At his door a general quavers,
"Sire, awake! Calamity!"
"What d'you want, good men, of me?
What calamity?" Dadon

Answers slowly with a yawn.
"Listen, sire – the cock is crowing:
In the city, fear is growing."
To the window – facing west,
See! the cockerel crows its best.
"Warriors all – no time to waste!
Every man to horse! Make haste!"
Off behind his elder son
Sets the army of Dadon.
Now the cock turns from the west,
Peace; the tsar returns to rest.

Seven days and not a word
From his army to be heard;
Was there, was there not, a battle?
Nothing to the capital.
Once again the cockerel crows.
Off a second army goes;
Now his younger son Dadon
Sends to save the elder one;
Soon the cockerel crows no more.
No word back, just as before!
Seven days again go past,
All the city is aghast;
Once again the cockerel crows;
Off Dadon's third army goes:

Whether or no it's for the best,
He leads this one toward the west.

Night and day his men of war
Marched till they could march no more:
Not a sign of battle found,
Bivouac or burial-mound.
Tsar Dadon, in puzzlement
As to what this mystery meant,
Led his men through passes high;
Seven days again went by.
And, upon the mountainside,
See! a silken tent is spied,
All in silence, all serene;
Close by, down a deep ravine
Lie the armies he has sent.
Tsar Dadon draws near the tent ...
Horror! Both his sons lie dead,
Armourless, with naked head,
Plunged in each the other's sword;
Back and forth upon the sward,
On the trampled bloody grass,
Their abandoned horses pass ...
Cried the tsar: "My sons – my sons!
Our two falcons both at once
Fallen to the snare! Oh woe!
Now my hour has come, I know."

All lamented with Dadon,
Valleys groaned with grievous groan,
And the mountain's heart was rent.
Suddenly the silken tent
Opened wide its flaps, and ah! –
Slowly, softly toward the tsar
Walked a maiden like the dawn,
Walked the Queen of Shamakhan.
As at sun the bird of shade,
He was mute before the maid,
Gazing long upon her eyes
He forgot his sons' demise.
She with bow and smiling face
Led him to her dwelling-place,
Seated him before her table,
There to feast all he was able;
Then she bade him lay his head
On a rich-brocaded bed.
Seven days passed by again;
Willing slave in her domain,
With the maiden queen Dadon,
Charmed, enraptured, feasted on.

Then the tsar, so long delayed,
With his warriors and the maid
Set off on his journey home
By the route that he had come.

All the way before him flew
Rumour true and far from true.
From the town gates with a shout
All the people hastened out,
Hailed the chariot from afar –
Ran behind the queen and tsar;
All were greeted by Dadon ...
Now he sees amidst the throng,
White in sage's hat and tunic,
All swan-white, his friend the eunuch.
"Father! What have you to say?
Closer ... Your petition, pray?"
Thus the wise man: "Let us clear
Our accounts at last, O Tsar.
Long ago you promised me,
For my services in fee
Whatsoever was my will
As your own you would fulfil.
Give me therefore, sire, the queen,
Give me the Shamàkhan Queen."
Answered Tsar Dadon like thunder:
"What is this I hear? – I wonder,
Has the Devil seized your wits?
So, I promised ... It befits
Age and wisdom to maintain
Limits. You – to play the swain?
Don't you know, then, who I am?

Ask for gold, a boyar's name,
Horses from the royal stud,
Half my kingdom if you would!"
"No, sire, none of these – the queen,
Give me the Shamàkhan Queen,"
Said the wise man to the tsar.
"Devil take you! You, I swear,"
Spat the tsar, "will never win her.
You torment yourself, you sinner –
Off, while you possess your soul!
Take away this doddering fool!"
Still the old man would persist;
Best not, though, with some, insist:
Now his brow the sceptre found,
Laid him out upon the ground
Stone dead. – All the city shuddered ...
No lament the maiden uttered:
"Ha-ha-ha!" and "He-he-he!" –
Unafraid of sin was she.
Tsar Dadon, alarmed the while,
Turned on her a tender smile;
On he drove towards the town ...
Came a gentle ringing: down –
Full in view of all the people –
Flew the cockerel from its steeple;
Met the chariot as it sped,
Perched upon the tsar's bare head,

Plumes a-ruffle, pecked his pate,
Up and off ... From lofty state
On the instant Tsar Dadon
Fell – and perished with a groan.
Wholly vanished was the queen,
Quite as if she'd never been.
This my tale, though not the truth,
Holds a lesson for our youth.

Notes

In these notes transliteration from the Cyrillic alphabet aims to render actual sounds. Spoken Russian stress is indicated.

Texts followed are those of the Complete Edition of the Works of Pushkin in seventeen volumes published by the Soviet Academy of Sciences, Moscow and Leningrad, 1937–59, reprinted by Voskresenye, Moscow (vol. 2, 1994; vol. 3, 1995; and vol. 5, 1994).

The Bridegroom

Page 9 stanza 1: *Natasha, disappeared; / ... Natasha reappeared*. Pushkin does not have this repetition, but I have taken the poem's overall balladic tendency to repetition as licence for it.

Page 10 stanza 2: In Pushkin's dynamic first four lines the ratio of verbs to other parts of speech is almost 1:1, as compared with 1:3 in my translation. In the last three lines my five *him*s keep rough parity with Pushkin's four.

Page 11 stanza 1: The last two lines show Pushkin's concentration: three out of four of his substantive words are rhymed, compared with three out of six in my translation.

Page 12 stanza 1: *linnet* in line 6 suits my translation as Pushkin's "swallow" (*kosàtke*) does his metre.

Page 14 stanza 1: Pushkin's onomatopoeia in the last four lines is unmatchable in translation. No less than six *s* and six *sh* sounds create the soughing of a dense wood: "*S tropìnki sbìlas' ya: v glushì / Nye slỳshno bylo ni dushì, / I sòsny lish' da yèli / Vershìnami shumyèli.*".

Page 15 stanza 1: *clop clop clop.* In a note to *Eugene Onegin*, Pushkin defends his use of words like *top* (the sound of horses' hooves) against reviewers' objections, citing their use in Russian folk literature. "These words are fundamentally Russian," he writes. "One should not interfere with the freedom of our rich and beautiful language."

The final couplet of this stanza is substantially repeated in the next stanza, with the rhyme-words *golubìtsa*, "pure creature", and *devìtsa*, "maiden", the last line consisting entirely of the weighty double noun *Krasàvitsa-devìtsa*, "Beauty-maiden" or "Maiden-beauty".

Page 16 stanza 1: In the final couplet, consecutive *a*, *u* and *r* sounds create a savage and sinister expression of the knifer's relish: "*Zladèy devìtsu gùbit, / Yey pràvu rùku rùbit.*" The exact phrase *pravu ruku* , "right hand", has already been heard in a subliminal pre-echo two stanzas previously; it has had to be lost in my translation "on his right".

Count Nulin

Page 19 lines 7–8: *his visage bears . . . proprietorial smile.* Pushkin's vowels are graphic: "*Yegò dovòl'noye litsò / Priyàtnoy vàzhnost'yu siyàyet.*" Literally: "His satisfied face / With pleasant importance shines." See also the second note to page 40 of *The Tale of the Golden Cockerel*.

Page 20 line 10: *Toasts the annihilating chase.* Pushkin exploits the long polysyllabic Russian adjective: his "toasts" comes at the end of the preceding line, leaving "annihilating chase" to occupy a whole line: "*Opustoshìtel'nyy nabyèg.*"

Page 20 lines 21–23: *"Natasha" . . . Natalya.* Play with nomenclature. "Natasha" is the name of wholesome "Russian" characters in Pushkin's earlier poems, as in *The Bridegroom*; later "Natalya" comes into its own, with more exalted associations, culminating in the "Madonna", Pushkin's wife. Here the more formal form is a veneer which goes with Natasha's "Europeanism", covering her true rural Russian self. For this analysis I am indebted to an essay by Boris Gasparov; see Afterword, note 12.

Page 23 line 12: *"Courage, allons!"* Nearly a dozen French phrases and names occur in *Count Nulin* in the Latin alphabet.

Page 23 lines 25 ff: *With store of hats ... / Handkerchiefs ...* These details are reminiscent of the "young philosopher"'s items of toiletry and dress as listed in the first chapter of *Eugene Onegin*, published on its own in the year *The Bridegroom* was written, 1825.

Page 24 line 2: *Guizot's new volume.* A work by this historian and conservative politician of the post-Napoleonic era could run up to to thirty volumes.

Page 24 lines 5, 6: *Béranger ... Paër.* The songs of Pierre Jean de Béranger, voicing the aspirations of the Parisian working class, were hugely popular throughout Europe, including progressive circles in Russia, for much of the nineteenth century. Ferdinando Paër's 43 operas include one, *Leonora*, that uses the same plot as Beethoven's *Fidelio*.

Page 24 lines 23–25: *Talma ... Mamselle Mars ... Potier*. Leading lights of the theatre of the Napoleonic era.

Page 25 line 6: *God grant we'll soon be educated*. Not yet. Alexander I's educational policies centred on the eradication of "subversive, un-Russian" ideas and "free thinking". Staff of Russia's five universities were sacked for their ideas of constitutional government.

Page 25 line 12: *Moscow Telegraph*. A popular literary review that included a pictorial supplement showing foreign fashions in clothes, furniture, etc.

Page 32 line 5: *everything*. If Pushkin's work on this poem had gone into a third morning he might have rhymed this line.

The Tale of the Golden Cockerel

Page 35 line 1: *Thrice-Ninth Clime*. Traditional form of words meaning "at the other end of the world", fairyland.

Page 35 line 14: *Men in thousands under arms*. Pushkin's "full line" here, consisting chiefly of a single monosyllable, "*Mnogochìslennuyu rat*'", is one of fourteen two-word lines in *The Tale of the Golden Cockerel*, which make up rather more than six per cent of all the lines and contribute significantly to the slow, measured rhythm of this tale. These two-word lines have an incantatory quality, "*Shamakhànskaya tsarìtsa* [or with its accusative -*uyu/u* ending]" occurring three times.

Page 36 line 1: *west*. Here and elsewhere Pushkin has "east", which doesn't suit the rhyme in English so well. There seems no particular significance in this point of the compass; it is simply that the next attack comes from an unexpected direction.

Page 37 lines 12–13: *"Now Tsar ... / What an easy life for you!"* These words (*"Tsàrstuy, lèʒha nà boku!"*, "Rule, lying on your side!") were removed by the censor on first journal publication.

Page 39 lines 20–22: *Back and forth ... horses pass.* Pushkin deliberately slows the tempo. "The image of grass, red with blood," the critic Valentin Nepomnyashchy has written, "grows to a monstrous size in close-up ... in a narrative shorn of colourful adjectives" (*Soviet Literature*, No. 1, 1987, Moscow, p. 117). The mode of repetition is now set up for the tsar's histrionics.

Page 40 line 2: *groaned with grievous groan*: Pushkin's repetition.

Page 40 lines 4–8: *Suddenly ... the Queen of Shamakhan.* In four and a half lines Pushkin has 22 *a* sounds, seven of them in a single climactic line, making the whole passage, as it were, one long gasp: *"Vdrug shatyòr / Raspakhnùlsya ... i devìtsa, / Shamakhànskaya tsarìtsa, / Vsya siyàya kak ʒaryà, / Tíkha vstrètila tsaryà."* I have thrown in *aw* along with *a* sounds, modest in number compared to Pushkin's performance.

Page 40 line 22: *Charmed, enraptured.* These words take up one of Pushkin's full lines: *"Okoldòvan, voskhishchòn".*

Page 42 line 13: *Best not, though, with some, insist.* Pushkin first wrote: "But with tsars it is bad to quarrel", and then changed "tsars" to "the powerful" (singular) before finalizing to, literally: "But with some it is costly to quarrel." Some bold post-communist Russian editors restore Pushkin's original line.

Page 43 lines 7–8: *This my tale ... our youth.* The censor, fearful of any possible political allusions, removed this concluding couplet.

Afterword

ALEXANDER PUSHKIN is central not only to Russian culture, but to Russian identity. He has given the Russians a language, a literature, and an inspirational demonstration of human claims against state power.

His verse stands out from that of his contemporaries of the Golden Age of Russian poetry – the first three decades of the nineteenth century – in three main ways. First, it makes poetry of plain spoken language. "Instead of the high-flown language of the gods," a listener to Pushkin's reading of his newly written *Boris Godunov* reminisces, "we heard language that was simple, lucid and everyday, and at the same time poetically enchanting!"[1] He popularized a new layer of words of subjective and emotional content modelled on French, such as *trogatel'nyy*, touching, *zanimatel'nyy*, absorbing, for which no equivalents had existed before in written Russian.

Secondly, and allied with the first point: Pushkin writes *lightly*. "Lightness," writes Andrey Sinyavsky, "is the first thing we get out of his works ... Before Pushkin there was almost no light verse [in Russia] ... And suddenly, out of the blue, there appeared curtsies and turns comparable to nothing

---

[1] The historian and journalist Mikhail Pogodin, writing in 1865. Quoted from *Pushkin on Literature*, edited and translated by Tatiana Wolff, revised edition reprinted London, 1998, p. 180.

and no one, speed, onslaught, bounciness, the ability to prance, to gallop, to take hurdles, to do splits ..."[2]

Thirdly, Pushkin writes *personally*. His lyric poems constitute a kind of emotional diary throughout his life; he writes of his African blood, his boredom in the countryside, insomnia, being with his nanny, carousing with friends – above all, the impact made on him by women.

His extensive and varied oeuvre fertilized the soil for Russian literature of the rest of the century and remained inspirational to Russian writers throughout the next. His completed work includes over 800 lyric poems, some dozen narrative poems, six verse fairytales, six verse plays,[3] a novel in verse, a novel in prose, six short prose tales, historical work, sundry prose, diaries and reminiscences.

Alexander Sergeyevich Pushkin was born on 26 May 1799 in Moscow. On his father's side he was descended from an old boyar family which had sunk into obscurity. On his mother's side he was the great-grandson of an (?) Abyssinian, Abram Petrovich Gannibal, who seems to have been the son of a prince, was brought to the court of Peter the Great as a boy, and attained eminence as a military engineer. Pushkin's was a neglected childhood; his pronounced African features may have reminded his mother of her bigamous father and turned her against her first son. The best times of his boyhood were spent in his father's extensive library of French literature, and listening to the conversation at literary evenings held at the house, attended by his verse-writing uncle and by leading writers of the day.

[2] Abram Tertz (Andrei Sinyavsky), *Strolls with Pushkin*, translated by C. T. Nepomnyashchy and S. I. Yastremski, New Haven and London, 1993, p. 51.
[3] The late drama *Rusalka* was revised and completed by Pushkin and is not the fragment it has always been taken to be. See the bilingual edition *The Return of Pushkin's Rusalka*, edited by V. Retsepter and M. Chemiakin, St Petersburg and London, 1998.

At the age of twelve Pushkin was admitted to the new Lyceum for gifted boys from cultured and noble families set up by Tsar Alexander I in a wing of his palace at Tsarskoye Selo outside St Petersburg. Tuition and board were free. Nearly one-sixth of all his lyric poems were written at the Lyceum, where he acquired his extraordinary fluency and ease in writing verse. He excelled in Russian and French literature but took little interest in other subjects, his performance in the final examinations getting him only a minor post in the Ministry of Foreign Affairs.

After leaving school, Pushkin spent three years in St Petersburg, to which his parents had now moved; he lived in a tiny room above their apartment on the Fontanka. His lifestyle resembled Onegin's (one imagines the latter as less dissipated). At a time of hardening autocracy, his reckless political verses would have landed him in Siberia had it not been for the efforts of high-placed friends, and he was sent to the more congenial South. During the six years spent there and on his mother's estate, Mikhaylovskoye, near the old north-west frontier town of Pskov, he took advantage of ideal conditions in which to write, and was spared the fate of his fellows in the Decembrist uprising of 1825 – Siberian or Caucasian exile at mildest.

Recalling Pushkin from exile in 1826 some months after Alexander's death and his own accession to the throne, Nicholas I extracted an undertaking from him not to write anything more "against the government", and, in order to avoid further difficulties, promised to be his personal censor, soon delegating this duty, however, to his secret police chief Count Benckendorf – not so well disposed towards the poet who was now the most popular literary figure in the country, the first Russian writer to earn a living by his pen.

Two years after his return from exile Pushkin met the sixteen-year-old beauty Natalya Goncharova; he married her three years later. Natalya had no interest in literature; her passion was the ballroom. She turned the head of the tsar. At the age of thirty-four Pushkin suffered the indignity of being appointed Gentleman of the Chamber, traditionally an eighteen-year-old's post, which made the couple's attendance at court balls obligatory.

Natalya met an immigrant Frenchman, a guards officer in Russian service, Baron d'Anthès. She flirted with him, and inevitably Pushkin was goaded into provoking a duel with d'Anthès, in which he was shot in the stomach, dying two days later (29 January 1837), at the age of thirty-seven.[4]

Pushkin and Natalya had four children; two of their grand-children, a brother and a sister, married grandchildren of Nicholas I.

The three verse narratives in this book, a tiny part of Pushkin's oeuvre, begin to give an idea of his enormous variety. Each belongs to a distinct genre of storytelling – ballad, full-scale narrative poem, folk or fairy tale.

Many of Pushkin's three dozen ballads are free translations or adaptations of foreign originals. Of his original works in the genre, *The Bridegroom* is one of a handful that attain the highest level. Pushkin uses the metrical form of the ballad *Lenore* by the German Romantic poet Gottfried Bürger (1774). Its story, based on the brief Scottish ballad *Sweet William's Ghost* (published in 1724), is of inconsolable grief for a dead lover, whose ghost takes the beloved on a long nocturnal ride to his grave-yard where she falls dead. Bürger uses the rich resources of the German language along with popular words such as *hopp* ("quick") and *tummle dich* ("get a move on").

Pushkin uses Bürger's eight-line stanza in *The Bridegroom*. Its combination of iambic tetrameter ("The thìrd night càme: in wìld disòrder") and trimeter ("They stìll were nòne the

---

[4] For the convoluted story of how Pushkin met his death, see Serena Vitale, *Pushkin's Button*, translated by A. Goldstein and J. Rothschild, London, 1999.

wiser") is dynamic in the extreme, constantly on edge and changing rhythm. Pushkin must have seen or read Bürger's ballad, at school (he studied German) or later.[5]

Pushkin wrote *The Bridegroom* in 1824–25, during his first year of exile at Mikhaylovskoye. The story of the merchant's daughter and her traumatic experience is his own, though it may be based on an oral source, perhaps told to him by his nanny, Arina Rodionovna, with whom he lived alone for two years at Mikhaylovskoye. It is told in the most oblique and subtle way, equally far from Bürger's head-on Romanticism and the popular balladry of Scottish and English tradition. Suspense is maintained from first stanza to last. Like other poems by Pushkin of this period and place – the well-known lyric "Winter Evening", for example – it draws richly on popular idiom. At the same time it is full of the most sophisticated effects, from dazzling onomatopoeia – the sound of wind-tossed fir-tree tops, the escalating din of a wedding feast – to eloquent repetitions, and echoes and parodies of *Lenore*. As so often, Pushkin has it two ways. He offers the reader the experience of a Romantic ballad, the sinister merging of dream world and reality.[6] But at the end, as the reader reviews what has actually happened in the story, the true nature of this highly original narrative emerges.

Count Nulin was conceived as a parody of Shakespeare's poem *The Rape of Lucrece*. "I thought," Pushkin wrote later,

> what if it had occurred to Lucrece to slap Tarquin's face? Maybe it would have cooled his boldness and he would have been obliged to withdraw ... Lucrece would not have stabbed

---

[5] Russian translations of *Lenore* published in 1808 and 1816 are not in Bürger's metre.

[6] Tatyana's dream (*Eugene Onegin* V.11–21, written a year later) will be in many a reader's mind to strengthen this experience.

herself ... Brutus would not have driven out the kings, and
the world and its history would have been different.

And so we owe the republic, the consuls, the dictators, the
Catos, the Caesars, to a seduction similar to one which took
place recently in our neighbourhood ...[7]

I was struck by the idea of parodying both history and
Shakespeare; I could not resist the double temptation and in
two mornings had written this tale.[8]

Pushkin takes the central event in Shakespeare's poem, the
rape, and mock-heroicizes it into a comic tale of rural life in his
favourite metre, the iambic tetrameter. He was working on the
fourth chapter of *Eugene Onegin* when he wrote *Count Nulin*,
and as John Bayley has observed, "we can imagine the heroine
and her husband [the small landowner and his bored young
wife, hungry for social contact] attending Tatyana's name-day
feast."[9] Sextus Tarquinius becomes Count Nulin, a travelling
dandy who spends a jolly evening in the house of the young
grass-widow and fumbles his way into her room after everyone
has retired to bed ... There are playful parodies of *The Rape*.[10]
Shakespeare's "lustful lord" becomes "our ardent hero".
Tarquin throws "his mantle rudely o'er his arm" and strikes a
light with his falchion; Nulin puts on "a striped silk dressing-
gown" and knocks down a chair in the dark. The very name
Nulin, based on the word *nul*, nil, parodies Sextus, Sixth.

But parody is not what the reader of this light-hearted
poem experiences and enjoys. Uppermost is a picture of the
delightful triviality of life in the country, a satirical but com-
pletely unmalicious portrait of two social types of the time, the

---

[7] Pushkin's friend Aleksey Vulf was said to have seduced the daughter of a
local priest.

[8] Note written by Pushkin around 1830. Quoted from Wolff, pp. 272–73.

[9] John Bayley, *Pushkin: A Critical Commentary*, Cambridge, 1971, p. 291.

[10] Most of those cited here are listed by A. D. P. Briggs, *Alexander Pushkin: A
Critical Study*, reprinted Bristol, 1991, pp. 104–06.

cosmopolitan fop and the minor landowner/his wife, with intimate detail of their lifestyle, material and moral. Earlier narrative poems by Pushkin, such as *The Prisoner of the Caucasus*, *The Fountain of Bakhchisaray* and *The Gypsies*, belong to Romantic tradition. The first readers of *Count Nulin* enjoyed its fizzing modernity of language, sensibility and characterization.

As so often with Pushkin, however, other concerns may lurk not far beneath the carefree surface. His above-quoted account of how he came to write *Count Nulin* continues with the cryptic sentence: "History does repeat itself strangely."[11] In the 1920s and '30s Russian critics began to suggest that *Count Nulin* does in some way relate vitally to Pushkin's serious concern with patterns of history at the time of writing (one month previously he had completed the historical tragedy *Boris Godunov*, which deals with cataclysmic historical events) and another Russian scholar has speculated that at this time "Pushkin pondered on history's laws and on the possibility of a chain of trifling accidents jeopardizing a great event."[12]

Early in December 1825, tucked away in Mikhaylovskoye, Pushkin heard of the death of Alexander I. Excitedly he looked forward to great changes in Russia and in his own life. He even set out illicitly for St Petersburg, but turned back when he encountered unlucky omens – he met a priest and a hare crossed his path. On the very day he would have expected to be in St Petersburg, he started to write *Count Nulin* instead, and finished it on the following day, when the abortive Decembrist uprising took place in the capital. But for the omens, he would have been there ("I would have been in the ranks of the rebels," he said to Nicholas I during the interview of 1826).

[11] Wolff, p.273.
[12] Yu. M. Lotman, in a contribution to the Yearbook of the Pushkin Commission, Leningrad, 1977, p. 90 (in Russian). Quoted by Boris Gasparov, "The Apocalyptic Theme in Pushkin's 'Count Nulin'", in *Text and Context: Essays to Honor Nils Åke Nilsson*, Stockholm, 1987, p. 17.

Recent criticism has tried Apocalyptic interpretation.[13] The year 7333 by the Old Russian chronological system, i.e. 1825, is supposed to have held allusions to prophecies of the coming of the Antichrist, after 1812 expected to come from Paris. In *Count Nulin* we have a Frenchified dandy journeying from Paris to the archaically, solemnly named "Petropole", who "curses holy Russia" and bears, among other articles from "the new Babylon", "the latest song by Béranger" (the Republican voice of the masses). He is likened to a "strange beast", a cat stalking a mouse, and in a last bestial image (implied) he is allied with the ominous hare as a potential quarry. But when Natalya, the healthy, rosy-complexioned, parodic rural personification of "Holy Rus", departs from the serious plot by boxing the Antichrist's ears, the prophecies are unfulfilled, nothing happens, Russia survives – as Russian autocracy and the status quo survived on 14 December, the likely outcome, as Pushkin might have felt in his bones beforehand, of any great political event in Russia in his day.

The Tale of the Golden Cockerel (1834) is the last of Pushkin's *skazki*, verse fairytales or folktales. Its storyline is based on Washington Irving's prose narrative "The Legend of the Arabian Astrologer" contained in *Tales of the Alhambra* (1832; Pushkin read a French translation of the same year), a popular compendium of history, legend and travel description.

Irving's is a flat narrative about a Moorish king of Granada, a good monarch who in his old age enlists the help of a wily astrologer who makes him a talisman, a bronze warrior, to warn him of approaching foes, and then by a trick takes from him his captive queen, who has limited magic powers, and disappears, leaving the king defenceless once more. From this material Pushkin fashions a closely wrought, electrifyingly dramatic tale. He makes the talisman, the golden cockerel, the

[13] See Gasparov; this paragraph largely summarizes his ideas.

central figure, and knits the other three, Tsar Dadon, the astrologer and the Queen of Shamakhan, into a dynamic relationship. He makes the tsar morally culpable, withholding the astrologer's promised reward and leading an empty-headed life of complete idleness. His astrologer is faithful and does the tsar real service. The queen's sinister aura of mystery and the supernatural dominates the second half of the narrative.

Pushkin's tale is drily, abstractly written, almost completely without descriptive physical detail. Its tone is lightly ironical and distanced, despite popular turns of phrase. Slight archaisms underline the general detachment. The language is so condensed that the prevailing effect is weighty and solemn; the gait of this tale is distinctly slower than that of Pushkin's other *skazki* written in the same metre. One Russian critic, finding a "'dissonance' between the literary genre and the style", writes that Pushkin is using the fairytale form "as a mask on the face of contemporary man."[14]

The Tale of the Golden Cockerel was written in autumn 1834, the beginning of the terrible final period of Pushkin's life. Chained to the capital by his humiliating court appointment when all he wanted was to write in the country, weighed down by debt, subjected to police spying (to his disgust, even his letters to his wife were opened) – during this year Pushkin became noticeably morose and wrote very little.

He had trouble, too, with the tsar. While his wife was recovering from a miscarriage brought on, so it was thought, by excessive dancing, he wanted to resign his post as Gentleman of the Chamber, but the tsar prevented him from doing so by threatening to withdraw permission for him to use the imperial archives to research the history of Peter the Great he was writing if he did. He was already disenchanted with Nicholas, who had broken his undertaking to be his personal censor.

[14] Valentin Nepomnyashchy, "A Few Words about the Tale [*of the Golden Cockerel*]", *Soviet Literature*, Moscow, No. 1 (466), 1987, p. 117.

In September he went alone to his estate of Boldino, east of Moscow. Here in previous years he had spent miraculously creative autumns, but this time he produced only *The Golden Cockerel*. It isn't hard to see a bitter caricature of Nicholas in the puffed-up Dadon, the autocrat who breaks his promises. Pushkin, in fact, removed a couple of pointed references from drafts. But in the wise eunuch-astrologer and his fate, an American scholar, Sona Hoisington, has suggested further autobiographical content.[15] She quotes a letter from Pushkin to his wife written in July: "I came within a hair's breadth of ... quarrelling with him ... If I quarrel with this one – I won't find another [tsar]." The fate of the astrologer might be interpreted as a warning to himself not to go too far with tsars – though to Soviet commentators, the tale's warning of the destructive potential of female beauty was always uppermost.

Hoisington sees evidence of an astrologer-cockerel-Pushkin nexus in the well-known sketch that Pushkin made for the cover of the fair copy of *The Tale of the Golden Cockerel* (see opposite). At top right, facing the bust of Tsar Dadon, is an ambiguous grotesque – presumably representing the astrologer – with "phallic-like features who appears to be making an obscene gesture at Dadon". Pushkin refers sardonically in correspondence of this time to his role as "court jester", and this autobiographical reference might be read in the depiction, in which, further, "the strong sexual overtones associated in the poem with the cockerel are transferred to the astrologer." Along with the cockerel's comb, I would add.

The cockerel is of course a common symbol for sexual potency, and here for creative potency. Hoisington suggests that the cockerel "is a symbol of Pushkin's masculinity, that

[15] S. S. Hoisington, "Pushkin's 'Golden Cockerel: A Critical Re-examination'", in *The Golden Age of Russian Literature and Thought*, edited by Derek Offord, New York, 1992, pp. 24–33, on which the rest of this and the next two paragraphs are based and from which quotations are made.

Pushkin's ink drawing on the cover of the notebook
containing the fair copy of *The Tale of the Golden Cockerel*

part of himself which he felt the tsar in real life had rendered impotent", observing that in the poem, when the astrologer speaks or acts on his own account, he is called "the wise man", but when he is the object of the tsar's action or perception he is called "the eunuch".

In these translations I have kept broadly to Pushkin's metrical schemes – since they work perfectly well in English – but not matched them exactly. I have not kept, for example, regularly alternating masculine and feminine (with a final unstressed or "weak" syllable) rhymes since the latter often strike a too heavily satirical note in English. This has inevitably meant that some variety of cadence has been lost. Further, since rhyme is easier in Russian than in English, I have allowed the occasional half and near rhyme in order to avoid the contortions that pursuit of full rhyme would have involved.

A key difference between the Russian and the English languages lies in word-length. Russian abounds in long sinuous words often extended by case and tense endings to five or six syllables; in English this number of syllables is rare except in the case of abstract nouns, whereas monosyllables are frequent. So keeping the same metre, the translator must either introduce extra English words to make up for the syllabic shortfall, or end up with fewer lines. I have generally chosen the latter course, and my translation of *The Golden Cockerel*, for example, has about seven per cent fewer lines than Pushkin's text.

The Russian language fits Pushkin's favourite metre, the iambic tetrameter (with x = unstressed syllable and $/$ = stressed: $x / x / x / x /[x]$), perfectly; *Count Nulin* is entirely in this metre. The polysyllables neatly and naturally fill the line, which commonly has only three words, noun, verb, and adjective or adverb, and not infrequently only two. Russian words, however long, never take more than one stress; unstressed syllables fall lightly on the ear several at a time, and the

Russian tetrameter, with four (notional) metrical stresses, usually ripples by with only two or three, the natural word-stresses. Russian, and Pushkin's, verse sounds more spontaneous and conversational than more heavily stressed English verse. I have allowed myself, after English tradition, the freedom to chop weak syllables from the metrical count and to reverse stress patterns (i.e. "*tum*-ti instead of ti-*tum*"), and have occasionally thrown in an extra syllable.

Pushkin's word-music, its physical basis the strong, highly coloured and dramatic sounds of Russian vowels and consonants, is often, of course, untranslatable. I have drawn attention in the end-notes to some unmatchable sounds.

Since Russians are still supposed to speak "the language of Pushkin", I have used language that I imagine he might have used, while not trying to sound either "period" or too pointedly of the present day.

Eugene Onegin apart, Pushkin's verse has not been well served by English-language translators. The rise of translation theory in recent decades has not so far been accompanied by the emergence of any substantial body of translation of Pushkin's other verse that has impressed as verse in English.[16] This book is an attempt to redress the balance with new translations of a selection of major poems, whether, as in the case of *The Golden Cockerel* and *Count Nulin*, a number of versions have previously appeared or, as in that of *The Bridegroom*, not so many.

A. W.

[16] From translators whose work I have read, I would single out D. M. Thomas (some of his versions of lyric poems in *The Bronze Horseman: Selected Poems of Alexander Pushkin*, 1982), Alan Myers (some lyric poems in *An Age Ago: A Selection of Nineteenth-Century Russian Poetry*, 1988), A. D. P. Briggs ("The Bronze Horseman" in *Alexander Pushkin*, Everyman's Poetry series, 1997), Ted Hughes, Seamus Heaney and Ranjit Bolt (respectively "The Prophet", "Arion" and "Tsar Nikita and his Daughters" in *After Pushkin: Versions of the poems of A. S. Pushkin by contemporary poets*, edited by Elaine Feinstein, 1999).

"The Angel list is a good thing" – Seamus Heaney

GENNADY AYGI
Selected Poems 1954–94
Bilingual edition with translations by Peter France
0 946162 59 x

The first substantial edition published in the English-speaking world of the work of one of the most original contemporary Russian poets. His free verse – disjunctive, subconscious, anti-rational – is at the confluence of avant-garde European modernism and the traditional culture of his near-Asiatic (Chuvash) homeland.

"A thought-provoking volume, and Peter France and the publishers have done all lovers of poetry a major service." – Andrew Reynolds, *Journal of European Studies*

PIERRE CORNEILLE
Horace
Translated by Alan Brownjohn; introduction by David Clarke
0 946162 57 3

A darkly gripping play about "power and the death of the heart" (George Steiner), which launched French classical tragedy (1640).

"Corneille's rhyming alexandrines have been superbly translated by Alan Brownjohn into a flexible blank verse which captures the nuances of meaning, but sounds as natural and flows as smoothly as prose." – Maya Slater, *Times Literary Supplement*

FERNANDO PESSOA
The Surprise of Being: Twenty-five poems
Bilingual edition with translations by James Greene and Clara de Azevedo Mafra
0 946162 24 7

Haunting poems written by Portugal's greatest modern poet in his own name – the most confounding of his personae – selected to show his evolution.

"The translators have succeeded admirably in the task of rendering this most brilliant and complex of poets into inventive, readable English." – *New Comparison*

RABINDRANATH TAGORE
Particles, Jottings, Sparks: The Collected Brief Poems
Translated by William Radice
0 946162 66 2

The first complete translation of Tagore's "brief poems" into English. These miniature fables, ironic quatrains, epigrams and fleeting verses jotted down throughout his life are central to the poetry and spiritual personality of the greatest of modern Indian writers.

"Tagore was deeply rooted in Indian tradition, deeper than any of his contemporaries or any Indian poet after him. It has been said that he was 'perhaps the last great poet of ancient India'. This is amply born out in Radice's new volume ... Non-Bengali-speakers have much to thank him for." – Khushwant Singh, *The Telegraph*, Calcutta

ANDREY BELY
The Silver Dove
Translated by John Elsworth
0 946162 64 6

The first modern Russian novel (1909), by an author whom Nabokov ranked with Proust, Kafka and Joyce. This first complete English-language translation was shortlisted for the Weidenfeld Translation Prize 2001.

"As well as an extraordinary work of literature, this is an important account of a historical moment ... Bely conveyed, above all, the attractiveness – ambiguous, suspect and yet overwhelming – of a fanatical mysticism cultivated in Russia before the Revolution ... John Elsworth has magnificently succeeded in recreating the flights and cadences of this work ." – Angela Livingstone, *Slavonica*

THEODOR STORM
The Dykemaster
Translated by Denis Jackson
0 946162 54 9

Der Schimmelreiter (literally "The rider on the white horse"), set on the eerie west coast of Schleswig-Holstein, is the story of a visionary young dyke official at odds with his community. A celebrated narrative tour de force.

"Translations of the high standing of this one are more than ever in demand." – Mary Garland, editor of *The Oxford Companion to German Literature* (third edition)

THEODOR STORM
Hanz and Heinz Kirch; *with* Immensee *and* Journey to a Hallig
Translated by Denis Jackson and Anja Nauck
0 946162 60 3

Three contrasting narratives by a writer who may claim parity with Thomas Hardy, two of them here translated into English for the first time. As in *The Dykemaster*, maps and detailed end-notes enhance enjoyment of fiction strongly rooted in time and place.

"The quality of these translations is outstanding; they contrive to read like natural English and yet capture beautifully the sense and rhythm of Storm's German." – *Forum for Modern Language Studies*

MIKHAIL ZOSHCHENKO
The Galosh and other stories
Translated by Jeremy Hicks
0 946162 65 4

These sixty-five short stories, nearly half of them translated into English for the first time, reveal one of the great Russian comic writers in their bitter-sweet smack and the fractured language of the argumentative, obsessive, semi-educated narrator-figure, trying hard to believe in the new Socialism.

"The translator's task is a high-wire act that Hicks performs with the utmost linguistic inventiveness." – Zinovy Zinik, *Times Literary Supplement*

MARINA TSVETAEVA
The Ratcatcher: A lyrical satire
Translated by Angela Livingstone
0 946162 61 1

Tsvetaeva's satirical narrative poem on conformism and material prosperity, using the story of "The Pied Piper of Hamlyn", first published in Prague in 1925-26, is widely considered her masterpiece. This uncompromisingly Russian explosion of clashing sounds, voices and rhythms, unpublished in Russia for forty years and published in entirety there only recently, has hitherto been known in English only in excerpts.

"In a finely tuned line of verse in translation, the style of the original ... not only shines through the dense layers of a foreign linguistic element but seems to stand on a level with it, as if two brothers were comparing heights together ... This was my experience when I read this translation of Tsvetaeva's *Ratcatcher*. Hats off to Angela Livingstone!" – Sergey Nikolayev, *Literaturnaya gazeta*, Moscow

"Angela Livingstone is unusually sensitive to cadence and form. This translation reads like a poem written in the English language." – Elaine Feinstein, *Poetry London*

" ... the very pinnacle of the art of translation: what translation of poetry should be but rarely is." – *Nina Kossman*

Publication: 2003

ALEXANDER PUSHKIN
Mozart and Salieri: The Little Tragedies
Translated by Antony Wood
0 946162 69 7

Pushkin's four "Little Tragedies", *The Miserly Knight*, *Mozart and Salieri*, *The Stone Guest* and *The Feast during the Plague*, are his most original contribution to drama and contain the finest blank verse in Russian literature. The longest of these highly condensed pieces is little more than 500 lines. Each works through a single moment to a powerful dénouement, and all are interlinked in a number of ways besides the extreme mental states of their protagonists, the miserly Baron, the envious Salieri, Don Juan and Walsingham, Master of Revels. On first publication twenty years ago, Antony Wood's translations were widely praised. In this third edition they have been revised, and the Introduction rewritten, in light of the experience of stage productions and readings and of current Russian interpretations.

On the first edition

"These versions are truly splendid." – Kyril Fitzlyon, *Sunday Telegraph*

"Antony Wood comes close to the translator's ideal." – Bernard Johnson, *The Tablet*